D0922309

Father's Day

A play

Eric Chappell

Samuel French — London
www.samuelfrench-london.co.uk

Rights of Performance by Amateurs are controlled by Samuel French Ltd, 52 Fitzroy Street, London W1T 5JR, and they, or their authorized agents, issue licences to amateurs on payment of a fee. **It is an infringement of the Copyright to give any performance or public reading of the play before the fee has been paid and the licence issued.**

The Royalty Fee indicated below is subject to contract and subject to variation at the sole discretion of Samuel French Ltd.

Basic fee for each and every
performance by amateurs   Code M
in the British Isles

The Professional Repertory Rights in this play are controlled by Samuel French Ltd.

The Professional Rights other than Repertory Rights are controlled by Bryan Drew Ltd, Mezzanine, Quadrant House, 80-82 Regent Street, London W1B 5AU.

ISBN 978 0 573 11557 8

Please see page iv for further copyright information

CHARACTERS

Henry Willows, serious-looking; 50s
Matthew Willows, Henry's son, jaunty, casually dressed;
   20s
Christine, punk/Goth in appearance; 16
Sue, Henry's ex-wife, attractive, well-rounded, fair-
   skinned; late 40s

SYNOPSIS OF SCENES

The action of the play takes place in the living-room of the
house of Henry Willows

ACT I
SCENE 1   A winter's evening
SCENE 2   Half an hour later

ACT II
SCENE 1   Midnight the same day
SCENE 2   Late the following morning

Time — the present

Other plays by Eric Chappell
published by Samuel French Ltd

Double Vision
Fiddlers Three
Haunted
Haywire
Heatstroke (Snakes and Ladders)
It Can Damage Your Health
Natural Causes
Rising Damp
Something's Burning
Summer End
Theft
Up and Coming

ACT I

SCENE 1

Henry Willows' living-room. A winter's evening

A bay window, R, *overlooks the front garden. A door,* UR, *leads off to the hall, kitchen and dining-room. Sliding doors,* L, *lead to the conservatory, and then to the back garden. On the back wall hangs a large, antique barometer. There is a fireplace in the* R *wall with an electric fire in the grate. A radiogram stands by the fireplace. Against the* US *wall stand a sideboard, a bookcase and a small table. On the sideboard are: a carriage clock, a drinks tray, various photographs, a fruit bowl containing four bananas, a Dresden figurine of a shepherdess and a Victorian miniature of a sheep dip. The bookcase is full of books and has a jar of loose change on it. There is a fishtank containing a single fish on the small table, with a container of fish food nearby.* C, *a three-piece suite faces* DS *with a coffee table before it. There is a lamp on the table*

When the CURTAIN *rises, classical music is playing on the radiogram. Henry Willows, a serious-looking man in his fifties, is seated listening to it. He is glancing at a paper and sipping a Scotch*

The doorbell rings. Henry frowns and ignores it. It rings again. He crosses to the radiogram and turns off the music

Henry (*glancing at the clock; muttering*) At this time of night? (*He moves to the fishtank and sprinkles fish food into it*)

The doorbell rings again

(*Addressing the solitary goldfish*) Don't they ever rest? I've been doubleglazed, I've been tarmacked, I've been photographed from the air. What more do they want? (*He shakes his head*) They know when you've got money. They can smell it. No matter how discreet you are, how modestly you live — they're there on the doorstep. (*He taps the barometer with a grim smile*) Well, if it's cold calling — they've picked the right night. It's down to freezing.

The doorbell rings again

(*Sighing*) You can't discourage some people.

He finishes his drink and exits into the hall

A moment later a light comes on in the conservatory and shines through the glass panels of the sliding doors

The shadowy figures of Matthew and Christine appear against the glass. Matthew is Henry's son, a young man in his early twenties. He is carrying a large haversack and is wearing a baseball cap at a jaunty angle. Christine is very young, a punk rocker with white make-up, dark hair, black clothes, black mittens, black fingernails, bondage jewellery, body piercings and tattoos; a very gothic look. She also has a haversack

Matthew opens the doors and comes into the room. He turns back to his companion

Matthew (*whispering*) Stay in there. I'll have to get him used to the idea ...

Christine moves back out of sight

Henry enters. He regards Matthew coldly, noting the large haversack. He moves towards Matthew

Matthew takes an uneasy step back into the conservatory

Matthew (*brightly*) Remember me?
Henry (*bleakly*) Yes.
Matthew I'm your son.
Henry I know.
Matthew (*after a pause*) Aren't you going to ask me in?
Henry No.
Matthew I'm Matthew.
Henry I know. I was at the christening.
Matthew Aren't you surprised to see me?
Henry No. I've been expecting it.
Matthew How could you? It's been years.
Henry I know how long it's been. You're not going to make a habit of this, are you?
Matthew I thought you'd be pleased to see me.
Henry Life's full of disappointments. You'll find that out. I did.

Henry tries to close the sliding doors, trapping Matthew's head and shoulders. Matthew moves back, leaving his foot in the doorway

Would you mind moving your foot? I've got a busy evening planned. Drop the catch on the way out. I don't want any more intruders.

Matthew But, Dad ——

Henry Don't call me that. You made your choice.

Matthew That was years ago ... (*He stops*) What am I supposed to call you?

Henry Mr Willows will do very nicely.

Matthew That was years ago, Mr Willows. Can't I come in? It's freezing out there.

Henry I'm not responsible for the weather.

Matthew I've got something to tell you.

Henry Well, tell me.

Matthew I'm frozen.

Henry Is that it?

Matthew No.

Henry sighs and reluctantly opens the door wider

Henry Well, since you've forced your way in, I'll give you five minutes.

Matthew comes in and puts the haversack down

But don't settle anywhere. And take that cap off.

Matthew Why?

Henry Because it's bad manners, that's why. Apart from that, I don't like them. They usually hide a pea-sized brain — close-set eyes, and a slack jaw.

Matthew (*removing the cap*) It's only a cap.

Henry It's the badge of the assassin, the thief and the intruder ... .

Matthew I wasn't intruding. You didn't answer the door.

Henry At this time of night, to some shifty individual with dodgy credentials? (*Broodingly*) You never get a close look at the card. They just waft it about and then sell you a dozen dishcloths while they case the joint.

Matthew You can always say no.

Henry I do — but they don't leave it at that. The last one tried to sell me a time-share. Took me an hour to get rid of him. Left in a fury. Spat in the flower bed. Did a wheel-spin on the drive and for the next three nights I get a pizza delivery I hadn't ordered. (*He returns to feeding the fish*)

Matthew Nice fish.

Henry stares at Matthew coldly

What do you call him?

Henry I don't call him anything. He's a fish.

Matthew I suppose he'd be happier in a pond.

Henry How do you know?

Matthew He looks sad.

Henry (*studying the fish*) They all look like that. Ever seen one grinning?

Matthew I hate to see anything caged.

Henry (*sharply*) It's not a cage — it's a tank. He arrived here in a plastic bag. After that, this is luxury. Caged!

Matthew I think I've said the wrong thing.

Henry You always did. (*He moves to the sideboard and pours himself another Scotch*)

Matthew watches enviously

I remember the last Christmas we were together. We couldn't afford much. I'd bought your mother a very nice roll-neck sweater. I was really proud of that sweater. We were driving back from the shops and I said: "I've got a lovely surprise for you, dear." And a small voice piped up from the back of the car. "It's a roll-neck sweater." Completely spoilt the surprise.

Matthew Was that me?

Henry Who else?

Matthew Sure it wasn't Julie?

Henry No. That was the same year you kicked my hubcaps in — the ones on the new Cortina.

Matthew I never kicked your hubcaps in.

Henry You mean it was never proved.

Matthew It was cousin Nigel.

Henry As far as I'm concerned the jury's still out.

Matthew You certainly know how to hold a grudge.

Henry I've had plenty of time to think about it.

Matthew (*after a pause*) I don't remember you calling her dear.

Henry Who?

Matthew Mum.

Henry Well, I did. I was very affectionate.

Matthew I don't remember that either. (*Pause*) Why were you expecting me?

Henry I thought my early retirement on a handsome pension and lump sum — together with the sale of Grandad Willows' house in Peckham and his generous legacy — may have shown up on the radar ...

Matthew I didn't come here for money.

Henry There's a novelty.

Matthew It's not a question of money. Have you ever asked yourself if I was happy?

Henry No, I've never asked myself that question. Why should I? Did you ask yourself if I was happy? You couldn't get out this house fast enough.

They left the *Titanic* with more dignity than you left this place. I was almost killed in the rush.

Matthew looks around for somewhere to sit

No, don't sit down. You'll only stiffen up.

Matthew We were very young! — and Terry was nice to us. He kept giving us sweets.

Henry (*scathingly*) Sweets! You were easily bought, weren't you?

Matthew You never gave us sweets.

Henry You left here without a backward glance. Even Julie.

Matthew That must have hurt.

Henry What?

Matthew Julie. She regrets it now.

Henry Does she?

Matthew I know she was special to you. Daughters are. She called you Dumpling — you called her Pumpkin.

Henry That was then — this is now.

Matthew You had plans for her. You wanted her to be a brain surgeon. You never had plans for me, did you?

Henry She was brighter than you were.

Matthew And she's got the looks.

Henry Has she?

Matthew Grown into a beautiful young woman. You'd be proud to be seen with her.

Henry Well, I don't have that privilege, do I?

Matthew Terry likes to be seen with her.

Henry Does he?

Matthew Now she's attractive to men …

Henry What?

Matthew In fact I don't like the way he looks at her …

Henry (*looking at Matthew suspiciously*) That's none of my concern, Matthew. And if you think this is having an effect on me, you're mistaken. Why have you come here?

Matthew I had a big row with Terry.

Henry What happened? Has he run out of sweets?

Matthew No. He's moan, moan, moan, all the time.

Henry I could have told you. He hasn't got my easy-going nature.

Matthew And he's sadistic. Always picking on Frank. Little things — like getting him to look down the garden hose, then turning the water on — or bursting his balloon with the end of his cigarette …

Henry (*staring*) He does that?

Matthew No wonder Frank wets the bed.

Henry He wets the bed? He never wet the bed.

Matthew He does now. It's always the children who suffer.

Henry Right. (*Pause*) So he's moan, moan, moan, is he?

Matthew He's no give and take.

Henry I don't know about give. He's got plenty of take — he took your mother.

Matthew She regrets it now.

Henry Another one! It must be a house full of regret.

Matthew He's always finding fault. Never leaves me alone. I got pissed off. So I packed a bag and left.

Henry Just a minute. What did you say?

Matthew I packed a bag and left.

Henry No, before that.

Matthew He's always finding fault.

Henry After that.

Matthew He wouldn't leave me alone.

Henry No. After he wouldn't leave you alone and before you packed your bag.

Matthew I don't remember.

Henry Oh, yes you do. That language may be acceptable where you came from, but not here.

Matthew They say it on television.

Henry You'll observe there's no television here.

Matthew Why not?

Henry Because television is now being run by delinquents.

Matthew What?

Henry It started in the seventies. That first generation of delinquents has now matured and is running television for the benefit of a second generation of delinquents, who are raising further delinquents.

Matthew So things can only get worse.

Henry Not necessarily. The next generation will probably die out through sexually transmitted diseases.

Matthew (*after a pause*) I think you've been on your own too long.

Henry Have I? There are thirteen-year-olds receiving treatment at the hospital. They're going into the clinic on skateboards.

Matthew We're not all like that, Dad.

Henry I said don't call me that.

Matthew You're right. It's a label. It gets in the way of a relationship.

Henry What relationship? We haven't got a relationship.

Matthew My friends call their fathers by their first names. It gets over the age gap. Helps them to become friends.

Henry I thought I'd made it clear that I don't want to become friends. Do you know what I'm going to do? Something I haven't done in years. I'm going to speak to your mother.

Matthew (*uneasily*) I wouldn't do that.

Henry Why not? (*Studying Matthew*) You're hiding something. You've got that sly look. Comes from your mother's side of the family. (*Pause*) Do you still go there for Christmas?

Matthew Yes.

Henry And do they still leave an empty chair for me?

Matthew No.

Henry No — your grandfather never liked me because I knew his secret.

Matthew What was that?

Henry That he's clinically insane. He tries to hide it but you can see it in his eyes. He knows I know — it makes him uneasy.

Matthew I'm not surprised.

Henry Does he still make all that fuss over the turkey?

Matthew Yes. We had a twenty pound one this year.

Henry You were lucky.

Matthew What did you have?

Henry Flu. I was in bed all over Christmas.

Matthew Oh. (*Pause*) Were you on your own?

Henry Yes.

Matthew I wish I'd known.

Henry Do you?

Matthew Did you get my card?

Henry No. Did you send one?

Matthew Yes.

Henry You've never sent one before.

Matthew I was never sure of the address. And I can never remember the name of the house.

Henry *Sunnybrook.*

Matthew (*frowning*) I don't remember a brook.

Henry There wasn't one. (*Pause*) It wasn't that sunny either.

Matthew I remember that.

Henry opens the door to the hall

What are you going to say?

Henry I'm going to beg them to take you back.

Matthew Suppose they won't.

Henry Then you can go to your granny and grandad — they may still have some of that turkey left ...

Henry exits

Matthew opens the sliding door

Matthew (*whispering*) Come in and get warm. He has all the radiators turned down, except in this room. That's why his tomatoes never ripen.

Christine enters. She whispers in Matthew's ear

No — it's going to be fine. I just have to win him over, that's all. (*He feels her hand*) You're frozen. (*He picks up Henry's glass*) Drink this. It'll warm you.

Christine hesitates

He won't mind. But don't smoke. He'll tell you all his friends who smoked are dead; the drinkers are too, but they didn't die as quickly. You look hungry. Have a banana. Build your strength up. (*He hands her a banana from the fruit bowl*)

Christine peels the banana and takes a bite during the following

Put the skin in your pocket. He'll like you — I know he will. Once he's got used to you. It's just that he's never accepted body piercing. When you first meet him — you'll find he can be dry, very dry, almost rude. He doesn't mean it — it's just his very dry sense of humour ... (*He listens*) He's coming back! Finish it in there.

Matthew pushes Christine back into the conservatory

Matthew drains Henry's glass, refills it from the decanter, and puts it back in place

Henry enters. He regards Matthew balefully

Matthew Did you make the call?
Henry Yes.
Matthew Surprised you haven't got a mobile.
Henry I don't have a mobile because I don't want my brains scrambled by radioactive forces.
Matthew Do you think that's going to happen?
Henry It already has. Do you know there are people getting phone calls in areas where it's been proved they can't receive signals? They are hearing voices, Matthew. Did you know that?
Matthew No.

Henry picks up the glass and studies it

(*Hastily*) Well, what happened?

Henry It was brief and to the point.

Matthew I'm not going back.

Henry That's fine. Your stepfather doesn't want you. He's changing the locks.

Matthew You spoke to him?

Henry Apparently your mother's out looking for you. (*Pause*) He said you threatened him with a knife.

Matthew I didn't.

Henry That's Grandfather coming out — we shouldn't be surprised.

Matthew I didn't threaten him. I was cutting some sandwiches and I made an angry gesture. I just happened to have the knife in my hand.

Henry He said you'd previously threatened him with a sweeping brush and a pair of garden shears. Did they just happen to be in your hand?

Matthew Yes.

Henry You seem to be making yourself very useful around there. I always remember you as bone idle.

Matthew He's bigger than I am.

Henry Do you think that's any excuse, you hooligan? That man took everything from me: my wife, my family, my happiness. Did I threaten him with a knife?

Matthew No — you pushed him through a plate glass window.

Henry (*frowning*) There was a scuffle in Woolworths, resulting in the incident you describe, it wasn't intentional. I am not a violent man. I am not confrontational. My trouble is I let people walk all over me.

Matthew I can't say I've noticed. I think I made a mistake coming here.

Henry No, your mistake was leaving there.

Matthew I won't be the only one …

Henry (*anxiously*) What do you mean?

Matthew There's Julie and Frank.

Henry There not coming as well, are they?

Matthew No.

Henry That's a relief.

Matthew Not yet …

Henry What?

Matthew Then there's poor Mum.

Henry (*cynically*) What about poor Mum?

Matthew I came home a few weeks ago — found her sitting in the dark — in tears.

Henry Really?

Matthew It was your wedding anniversary …

Henry Oh, yes …

Matthew She had your photograph.

Henry Did she?

Matthew She had been trying on her old wedding dress.

Henry If she had been trying to squeeze into that, no wonder she was in tears.

Matthew She said: "What happened, Matthew? What went wrong? Where did it all go?"

Henry She said that?

Matthew I told her it was too late for regrets — that you were divorced. Do you know what she said? "We're still married in the eyes of God, Matthew."

Henry She brought God into it? That's a surprise. She hasn't been to church since the christenings.

Matthew Don't you remember your anniversary?

Henry No. If I was going to celebrate anything, it would be the divorce.

Matthew You can't celebrate a divorce.

Henry Why not? You don't celebrate the outbreak of war — you celebrate the peace. And it's been very peaceful around here — until you came.

Matthew If you feel like that, why are you drinking a little too much?

Henry I'm not!

Matthew Is it to deaden the pain?

Henry There isn't any pain!

Matthew (*motioning to the sideboard*) And why have you replaced her photo with a bowls team?

Henry For the simple reason that the bowls team hasn't been unfaithful to me. And she wasn't trying on her wedding dress, Matthew, because it was hired. Do you think I was mad enough to buy a dress you can only wear once — or in your mother's case, twice? (*He reaches for the decanter and frowns*) You've been at this Scotch.

Matthew No.

Henry Listen, I live alone. I have regular habits. I drink moderately. I know how much should be in this decanter on any day of the week. And the level has fallen ...

They study the decanter

Matthew Perhaps it's evaporated.

Henry Let me smell your breath. Not too close. (*He sniffs near Matthew*) Just as I thought. You've been drinking. It's amazing. I haven't seen you in years and one night, without warning, you burst into my home. And if that's not bad enough, I find you swear, you drink, you take things that don't belong to you, you're a stranger to the truth — and you're handy with a bread knife. And all that in the first half an hour. Have you any idea what a weekend would be like?

Matthew Were you thinking of just the weekend?

Henry No! (*The fruit bowl catches his eye*) And you've had a banana.

Matthew I haven't.

Henry There were four bananas in that bowl when I left this room. Now there are three. You've taken a banana and what's worse you've lied about it.

Matthew I'm not lying. (*After a hesitation*) Chris had the banana.

Henry Oh. So you have a companion?

Matthew Yes.

Henry And where is Chris?

Matthew In the conservatory.

Henry Finishing off the tomatoes, I suppose.

Matthew We haven't eaten all day.

Henry So he promptly lifts a banana. He could have asked — I'd have given him one.

Matthew Chris isn't a he. It's Christine.

Henry (*sharply*) You've brought a girl here?

Matthew Yes. That's the reason I came.

Henry Is it?

Matthew They don't approve of her.

Henry And you think I will?

Matthew You're not like them.

Henry I'm not?

Matthew You're strict, but, my God — you're fair.

Henry And do you think I need to be fair where Christine's concerned?

Matthew No, but she's encountered a lot of prejudice.

Henry Why the prejudice?

Matthew I don't know.

Henry Well, is she coming out from there — or is she happier amongst plants?

Matthew I thought I'd prepare you.

Henry I'm prepared.

Matthew opens the sliding door

Matthew Christine …

Christine enters

This is Christine …

Christine nods in Henry's general direction. She remains silent, head lowered. Henry stares incredulously as he takes in the sight. Christine whispers in Matthew's ear

(*To Henry*) Do you think Christine could use the bathroom?

Henry First door at the top of the stairs.

Matthew First door at the top of the stairs, Christine.

Christine exits

Henry What was that?

Matthew (*coldly*) Do you mean Christine?

Henry Christine? Thank God. I thought it was the third witch out of *Macbeth*.

Matthew You're as bad as Mum.

Henry Because she doesn't approve? Have you thought your mother may have a point? She's got more tattoos than a navy stoker and she appears to be held together with safety pins.

Matthew That's body piercing.

Henry Is it?

Matthew You shouldn't go by appearances.

Henry Oh? Then why doesn't your mother approve?

Matthew She says she's too young.

Henry How does she know? How old is she — beneath that layer of silt?

Matthew Sixteen.

Henry Sixteen! She's only sixteen! No wonder your mother doesn't approve.

Matthew That's not the reason. No-one's ever been good enough for her son. You know that. She's frightened of losing me.

Henry Are you sure? I don't think she's frightened of losing you — I think she's frightened of gaining her.

Matthew She may be only sixteen but she's old for her years — and intelligent. She's at college. She's doing catering.

Henry You mean they let her near food?

Matthew She's very good with food. She could do us supper.

Henry What does she use — a cauldron?

Matthew You can sneer but she'll make a wonderful wife.

Henry Wife?

Matthew We're getting married.

Henry What!

Matthew We want your approval.

Henry You've never wanted my approval before — why now? Why not your mother's approval?

Matthew I've told you — she doesn't approve.

Henry (*after a pause*) Can she talk?

Matthew Of course she can talk.

Henry I didn't hear her.

Matthew She's shy.

Henry Dressed like that! And she's shy! How are you going to get through the wedding service? They'll never hear her. You can't say, "She does." It's not legal.

Matthew She lacks confidence. I'm giving her that.

Henry You can't change people, Matthew. What she is now is what she will be — only worse. I know. I tried to change your mother.

Matthew Mum can talk.

Henry Yes — the problem there was stopping her. What does her father do?

Matthew Does it matter?

Henry Of course it matters. I'm not paying for the reception. Does he have any money?

Matthew It's always money, isn't it? Well, it doesn't matter because he doesn't approve of me.

Henry (*in mock surprise*) Really?

Matthew He preferred Simon. Boy next door. Got a good job at Nationwide. Drives his own Mondeo. So there won't be any money. Does it matter?

Henry Of course it matters.

Matthew Did Mum's dad have any money?

Henry If he did, he kept it a secret. I had to ask his permission. You did in those days. He had the air of a man passing me a counterfeit ten pound note. Pretending to be reluctant but at the same time knowing he was getting the best of the bargain. He was on an economy drive at the time. He'd had the phone taken out, the dog had been put down — your mother was next on the list. His only disappointment was that we didn't elope and save on the reception. His final words were, "Don't expect anything from me — she comes as she is." And that man's word was his bond.

Matthew He never gave you anything?

Henry I tell a lie. Years later he relented, and gave me a burnt-out power drill.

Matthew Then you can appreciate my position. I won't get any help from Christine's father. Simon was a better prospect. But they quarrelled. She came to me on the rebound.

Henry You should have ducked.

Matthew Look. Just get to know her. That's all I ask.

Henry How am I going to get to know her? You can't stay here.

Matthew Why not?

Henry There's not room for two of you — and if you think you're sharing …

Matthew I wasn't suggesting anything of the sort. There are two other bedrooms.

Henry The little bedroom's full of apples.

Matthew We could move them.

Henry They bruise easily. (*He moves to the hall door*) How long is she going to be up there?

Matthew She's probably putting on her make-up.

Henry Isn't she wearing enough? (*Pause*) Ever seen her without it?

Matthew Why?

Henry You could be in for a shock.

Matthew If you insist on taking this attitude, I think we'd better go.

Henry Let me tell you something, Matthew. It's not the spider that catches the fly — it's the web. Now you can't blame the fly, he doesn't see the web — but we do. In fact, that's what we fall for.

Matthew (*staring*) What web?

Henry The web of deceit, of perfume and flattery, of make-up and come-hither looks. That's what we fall in love with, the web not the spider.

Silence

Matthew I think you've become disillusioned,

Henry (*drily*) You've spotted that, have you?

Matthew picks up his haversack

Where will you go?

Matthew I don't know. We'll sleep rough. A waiting-room — or someone's car.

Henry What!

Matthew I know how to get into them — and start them.

Henry Well, I'm glad your education hasn't been entirely wasted. Who taught you that? Those friends who call their fathers by their first names? (*He opens the hall door*)

Matthew Where are you going?

Henry To get in touch with your mother.

Henry exits

Matthew listens at the door and then moves to the sideboard. He searches the drawers and finds a picture of his mother in the bottom one. He smiles and puts the picture out in place of the bowls team. He searches further in the drawers and finds a bundle of letters which he studies with some amusement and then pockets. He empties the jar on the bookcase and pockets the loose change. He finishes Henry's Scotch then studies the decanter. He fills it up from the water jug, giving it a generous level

There is the sound of a car arriving outside. Hearing this, Matthew moves to the window and peers out into the road. There is a moment's pause

Sue, Matthew's mother, enters from the conservatory. She is an attractive, rounded, fair-skinned woman in her late forties. She is wearing a topcoat and carrying a large shoulder bag

Moving silently as if afraid of detection, Sue creeps up behind Matthew and cuffs him

Matthew Mum! You still care.

Sue (*in a low voice*) I told you not to come here. The car's outside — get in it.

Matthew What about Christine?

Sue Where is she?

Matthew In the bathroom.

Sue Where's your father?

Matthew On the phone — trying to get you.

Sue I don't want to speak to him.

Matthew Is the memory still painful?

Sue Yes. I still wake up screaming.

Matthew You don't mean that, Mum — and neither does he. Look at this room. It's almost a shrine. Your picture, the little Dresden shepherdess, the Victorian miniature, the "Sheep Dip". He's kept them all. Everything that reminded him of you.

Sue Yes ... (*She stuffs the items mentioned into her bag during the following*)

Matthew (*staring in horror*) What are you doing?

Sue These are mine. They were in the settlement. He said he couldn't find them — that they'd gone missing. Missing! (*She looks at the bookcase*) And the *Oliver Twist* — early edition — illustrated by Cruickshank. (*She snatches the book from the shelf*)

Matthew You can't do it, Mum. It'll break his heart.

Sue I paid for these with my own money. Go and get Christine. I'll take these to the car. (*She makes to move away but sees the clock and stops*) The carriage clock with the Westminster chimes! He swore it was lost. That's mine.

Matthew It's not even keeping proper time.

Sue That's because he probably buried it in the garden until the fuss died down. (*She stuffs the clock into her bag*) Don't look at me like that. I sat for hours in draughty salesrooms to get these. (*She moves towards the conservatory door*)

Henry enters

Henry Your mother's still out looking for you ... (*His voice dies away as he catches sight of Sue*)

Sue clutches the bag defiantly

(*Smiling coldly*) Well, well, well ...

Sue What does that mean?
Henry What?
Sue Well, well, well?
Henry I'm surprised to see you, that's all. You said you'd never come back.
Sue I came for Matthew. Matthew, wait in the car.
Matthew What about Christine?
Sue I'll bring Christine.

Matthew exits

Henry pours himself a drink

Henry Well, well, well …
Sue Don't keep saying that. I had to come.
Henry Why?
Sue I couldn't let him make the same mistake I did.
Henry What mistake was that? The first or the second?
Sue What's he been saying?
Henry Nothing.
Sue She's totally unsuitable.
Henry (*enjoying himself*) I thought they made a perfect couple.
Sue You can't be serious. Have you seen her? What did you think?
Henry Enchanting.
Sue She should be in a circus! She'll hold him back.
Henry Why — is he going somewhere?
Sue One day he'll have a career. Perhaps bring the boss home for dinner.
  What's he going to think when Coco the Clown serves up the roast in
  mittens?
Henry She's doing catering.
Sue I know she's doing catering!
Henry I think he's done rather well.
Sue What!
Henry After all, he's not much of a catch. He comes from a broken home,
  he hasn't finished college — they'll have to burn it down to get him out of
  there.
Sue I knew you'd be no help. I told him not to come here. If Terry knew where
  I was …
Henry Where does he think you are?
Sue I've no idea but if he thought I was here — he'd go mad.
Henry Why?
Sue (*after a hesitation*) He doesn't trust you.
Henry (*coolly*) In what regard?
Sue You know …

Henry Oh. He thinks I may not be able to resist you?

Sue I didn't say that.

Henry I think he's being most unreasonable. After all, I trusted him.

Sue That's why. I suppose.

Henry Doesn't he know I was trapped into matrimony?

Sue Trapped!

Henry That I had to make an honest woman of you.

Sue Trapped! You seduced me.

Henry Seduced you. That's a phrase you don't hear very often these days.

Sue You were older.

Henry You were born older. You led me on.

Sue Led you on? That's a phrase you don't hear very often these days.

Henry There was a theory in my day, that if a woman was good enough to sleep with, she was good enough to marry. Well, you certainly disproved that theory.

Sue I'd forgotten how objectionable you could be.

Henry Tell Terry — it'll relieve his worries. You can also tell him that my self-control has improved over the years. I feel no desire to throw myself on top of you. You've put on weight.

Sue Well, you didn't expect me to look like my picture.

Henry What? (*He moves to the sideboard and discovers Sue's picture*) That shouldn't be there.

Sue Shouldn't it?

Henry That was in a drawer — the bottom one.

Sue But you kept it.

Henry You're lucky I didn't draw a moustache on it. Matthew must have found it. He hasn't changed. Remember how he loved us to go out so that he could search the house? I think he was trying to find out if he'd been adopted.

Sue You mean he hoped he'd been adopted. (*Pause*) Well, what are we going to do?

Henry We? It's a little late for we. Now I suggest you collect the ravishing Christine and return to the happy home. (*He taps the barometer*) She's in the bathroom applying yet another coat. And watch the roads, they could be icy.

Sue I'll never come here again.

Henry You've said that before.

Sue moves towards the hall. The clock in her bag begins to chime. Sue and Henry stare at each other

What was that?

Sue What?

Henry (*looking at the sideboard*) Where's my clock?
Sue My clock.

Henry checks the room. Sue heads for the door. Henry stops her

Henry What's this? (*He peers into the bag*) The carriage clock with the
   Westminster chimes! The Dresden shepherdess! The Victorian miniature!
   I'm being robbed!
Sue You're not. They're mine — and you know it.
Henry They were yours. And if you hadn't been in such a hurry to leave you
   could have taken them. But now they're mine — possession being nine
   points of the law.
Sue That doesn't make them yours. They were in the settlement ...

They struggle over the bag during the following

Henry That was years ago. We're outside the statute of limitations ...
Sue You always had the mind of a solicitor's clerk. They're mine.

They pull back and forth. Sue aims a kick at Henry but misses

Henry You're losing your touch. You never missed in the old days. The
   weight must be slowing you down ...

*They wrestle the bag to the ground. The contents roll on the floor. They get
down on their hands and knees, struggling for them*

   *Christine enters. She looks down at them in alarm. She gives a low moan
   and slumps to the floor*

*Sue and Henry look at each other in surprise. They stare over the sofa at the
fallen Christine*

   Matthew enters

CURTAIN

SCENE 2

The living-room. Half an hour later

When the CURTAIN *rises there is the sound from offstage of a car failing to
start; this sound stops during the following. Henry is on stage, positioning the*

clock on the coffee table. He listens hopefully for the tick and sighs. He checks the shepherdess on the sideboard and sighs again. He moves to the sideboard and pours himself a drink. He sips his drink and frowns, then holds up the decanter and studies the colour of the liquid in it

Sue enters uneasily from the hall with her bag

Sue The car won't start.

Henry Well, well, well.

Sue I know it's been a long time, but the "well, well, well," is new, isn't it?

Henry I'm surprised, that's all.

Sue I'm not. It's an old car.

Henry So he hasn't exactly kept you in luxury.

Sue I didn't have a car when I was here.

Henry There are too many cars. When I look out during the rush hour I can see the trees on the road wilting.

Sue Oh. I didn't know I was saving the planet when I stood at the bus stop in the pouring rain. I thought it was because you were mean.

Henry (*angrily*) I'm not mean. If you're looking for meanness, try your father. One burnt-out power drill in twelve years.

Sue And what about your father? Didn't he drive his dead mother all the way from Torquay to save on the funeral expenses?

Henry That's a lie! She died on the way home.

Sue Well, there's no point in arguing with each other. What are you going to do?

Henry Do?

Sue About the car?

Henry I don't know anything about cars. Try Matthew. He can start cars, often without the owner's consent — or so he tells me.

Sue Where is Matthew?

Henry With the ravishing Christine. Holding her hand.

Sue We shouldn't leave them alone together.

Henry Why not? They want to get married.

Sue He told you that?

Henry Yes.

Sue Then it's probably too late.

Henry What do you mean?

Sue (*producing the predictor from a pregnancy detector kit from her bag*) I found this in his bedroom a few days ago … Do you know what it is?

Henry studies the object in Sue's hand

Henry Let me see … Looks like a game of chance …

Sue You could say that.

Henry I suppose you have to get the ball in the plastic tube. There's a mirror — not sure what that's for. Oh, and two symbols — plus and minus — probably to indicate if you've won or lost …

Sue Precisely. It's a pregnancy testing kit.

Henry What! And they're together up there! (*He heads for the door*)

Sue I think it's too late to close the stable door, Henry.

Henry I wasn't going to close the stable door. I was going to have a word with the horse.

Sue It's a little late for that, too.

Henry Well, what am I supposed to do? I was sitting here minding my own business when you arrive like the ghost of Christmas past in pursuit of your delinquent son.

Sue He's not a delinquent!

Henry I'm not responsible for your life. I can't help it if you're worn down by poverty, that you've put on weight, and that you're driving a car fit for the scrap heap. They are your problems. Just because I've come into a little money …

Sue I didn't know that.

Henry Don't tell me you didn't send for a copy of the will.

Sue I did not.

Henry You surprise me. You must be slipping.

The phone begins to ring, off, in the hall. They look at each other

Sue My God! If that's Terry — don't say I'm here. He'll go mad.

Henry Why? Are you afraid of him.

Sue No.

Henry You were never afraid of me. Does he knock you about?

Sue No!

Henry Pity. I always thought it might improve you.

Henry exits into the hall

Sue listens at the hall door

The door opens suddenly and Matthew enters

Matthew He's talking to Terry.

Sue Oh God. It's just one thing after another.

Matthew What's the matter?

Sue The car won't start.

Matthew I'll take a look at it. (*He turns to leave*)

Sue (*stopping him*) How's Christine?
Matthew She's resting.
Sue She tires very easily, doesn't she?
Matthew She's not very strong.
Sue But she's all right? She's not sick or anything? I mean she did faint.
Matthew That was shock.

Sue moves to the coffee table, followed by Matthew. Sue places the predictor on the table

Sue So we've got nothing to worry about?

They both study the predictor

Matthew Where did that come from?
Sue Out of a cracker! Where do you think it came from? (*Pause*) I just want to know what it is.
Matthew I'm not sure. It's not mine. I think you have to get that ball into ——
Sue Don't try that with me! (*She aims a cuff at him*) She's pregnant. Isn't she?
Matthew I don't know.
Sue Well, if you don't know, no-one does. You've heard of cause and effect. Well, you're the cause and that's the effect.
Matthew It's not absolutely definite.
Sue How definite is it?
Matthew Well, there's a strong possibility that she may be with child.
Sue (*aiming another cuff*) Don't try and be funny. How much of a possibility?
Matthew Well, something that should have happened — hasn't happened.
Sue Don't you mean something that shouldn't have happened has happened? She's sixteen, Matthew.
Matthew But she's mature for her years.
Sue She is now! You realize you've ruined your life. Why couldn't you have waited? You couldn't, could you? Ever since I can remember you've always opened your presents before your birthday —— and you're still doing it!

Henry enters

Henry He wants to speak to you.
Sue (*alarmed*) You told him I was here?
Henry I wasn't going to lie for you. Why should I? If you have domestic problems ...

Sue I don't have domestic problems. You could have said I'd left. I was leaving.

Henry But you haven't. And I don't think there should be secrets between man and wife, do you? But what am I saying? Of course you do. You've done it before. (*Pause*) He's waiting to speak to you …

Sue marches angrily into the hall

Henry picks up his drink and sips it thoughtfully. Matthew watches him. Henry studies the decanter

A strange thing's happened to this Scotch.

Matthew Has it?

Henry Yes. The level's gone up.

Matthew I've added to it.

Henry Have you?

Matthew From a miniature.

Henry A miniature?

Matthew I always carry a miniature in this weather.

Henry I didn't know that.

Matthew Keeps the cold out.

Henry That was very kind of you.

Matthew I didn't want you to think I was freeloading.

Henry No. It's not very strong, is it?

Matthew It's a very subtle blend.

Henry Subtle! It's water. You've watered the Scotch, haven't you?

Matthew (*after a pause*) Yes. I was worried about you.

Henry (*staring*) Worried about me?

Matthew You're drinking too much.

Henry So you decided to water the Scotch?

Matthew At least that way you won't become an alcoholic.

Henry I'm not becoming an alcoholic! You've got an answer for everything, haven't you? Well, I hope you've got an answer for what's happening upstairs. I understand from your mother that you may have — how can I put this delicately — anticipated the lawful rites of matrimony.

Matthew What?

Henry That you're going to be a father. (*He brandishes the predictor*) I know what this is. I am abreast of medical developments. Well, what's your answer to this little situation?

Matthew Marriage.

Henry You've ruined your life.

Matthew That's what Mum said. You're both the same. You're only worried about what people may say. Well, I'm not. Words can't hurt you.

Henry To say that, Matthew, is to ignore the depth of mental scarring. How do you think I felt when the judge in chambers referred to me as a father lacking in warmth and understanding. Do you think it was easy facing my neighbours after that?

Matthew I don't care about neighbours.

Henry You haven't got any! You're a nomad!

Matthew Right. That's me. A free spirit. I believe in personal freedom.

Henry And what happens when your personal freedom conflicts with my personal freedom?

Matthew What do you mean?

Henry Suppose you're in the garden enjoying your personal freedom by playing your transistor at full blast which effects my personal freedom to sit in the garden and enjoy the birdsong. What's going to happen?

Matthew I don't know.

Henry I approach you — wearing my mantle of authority — and drop your transistor into the water butt. So much for your personal freedom.

Matthew Mantle of what?

Henry Authority.

Matthew Why do you get to wear the mantle of authority?

Henry Because I'm older and wiser — and it's my house.

Matthew So you're always going to wear the mantle of authority.

Henry No. The word mantle means my authority is temporary — the mantle can be removed.

Matthew When?

Henry When you detect signs of approaching senility and you shove me into an old people's home.

Matthew I'd never do that to you.

Henry Wouldn't you? You've been searching the sideboard. You were looking for the will, weren't you?

Matthew No. I hope you have a long and happy life; we all do.

Henry Who's we?

Matthew Julie, Frank and me. A long and happy life, but when it does draw to a peaceful end — we do hope to be mentioned …

Henry (*appalled*) You three sit around talking about my will?

Matthew Not exactly. But we have to think about the future — and now I have responsibilities.

Henry You really are going to marry her?

Matthew Well, you married Mum after you knocked her up.

Henry Knocked her up! That's your mother you're talking about. And I didn't.

Matthew My arithmetic was never very good, Mr Willows, but I couldn't help noticing that your wedding anniversary was a little too close to my first birthday for comfort.

Henry You were premature.

Matthew Don't you mean you were? Didn't you "anticipate the lawful rites of matrimony"?

Henry (*uneasily*) No.

Matthew I don't mind being a love child.

Henry There was nothing lovable about you.

Matthew Is that why you never hugged me?

Henry Of course I hugged you.

Matthew I don't remember. They say it's good for children to be hugged.

Henry Who says?

Matthew Psychiatrists.

Henry Then let the psychiatrists hug them. And let me tell you something else. I don't know what you're planning but she's not having the baby here. I'm not going through all that again. I've only just got the stains out of the carpet from the last time ...

Matthew Why are you so angry? Do you think you're too young to be a grandfather?

Henry No — I think you're too young to be a father — and she's certainly too young to be a mother.

Matthew Well, that's for nature to decide. We're in her hands now.

Henry (*slowly*) Not necessarily. (*Pause*) There is an alternative ...

Matthew What?

Henry You're not going to like this. And it's only a suggestion. But in view of her age they may consider — an abortion.

Matthew No!

Henry I said you wouldn't like it.

Matthew You couldn't do that to a defenceless baby.

Henry It's not a baby.

Matthew It is. In a few weeks it will be sucking its thumb. Could you do that to a little creature sucking its thumb?

Henry It was only a suggestion.

Matthew It was a rotten suggestion.

Sue enters

Sue What was?

Matthew An abortion.

Sue That's your father for you — always ready with a solution.

Henry It was only a suggestion.

Matthew I'm shocked.

Sue I'm not. He wanted to do that to you.

Matthew What!

Henry We discussed it, that was all.

Sue You bought me a bottle of gin. You'd never done that before.

Matthew You wanted to kill me?

Henry I didn't know you.

Matthew You didn't intend to. I always knew I wasn't loved.

Sue You were loved. See what you've done, Henry?

Henry What I've done! You were loved, damn it. But you don't know what it was like in those days — the scandal, the stigma. An unmarried mother — they wouldn't have let her run a Brownie pack.

Sue I didn't want to run a Brownie pack.

Henry We had no choice. We had to get married.

Sue No choice!

Matthew You mean there was no affection?

Henry Of course there was — but we had to do what was right.

Sue Right!

Matthew Well. That's what I'm doing.

Henry But you don't have to — not now. Have you thought of adoption?

Matthew (*bitterly*) Often — but who'd adopt me at my age?

Sue You see what you've done, Henry? We do love you, Matthew. He can't say it because he's an anal retentive.

Henry What!

Sue But I'm not like that. I'm loving.

Matthew (*smiling*) I know, Mum. I've seen your letters … (*He takes the bundle of letters from his pocket and places them on the coffee table*)

Henry and Sue stare at the letters. During the following, Sue picks them up and studies them

Sue Where did these come from?

Matthew From the sideboard. He kept them.

Henry They're private property!

Sue You kept my letters?

Henry Yes.

Sue Why?

Henry Evidence. So that when you'd finished telling everyone how much you loathed me — I could produce these as evidence to the contrary.

Matthew Are you sure? You couldn't destroy letters like these, they're beautiful …

Henry (*to Sue*) Give them back — they're mine.

Sue I wrote them.

Henry They're addressed to me. That makes them — *ipso facto* — my property.

Sue I knew you'd have a legal argument. (*Looking at the letters*) I wrote these? My God! Green ink!

Matthew Is that the one where you say: "I long to be with you tonight and feel your strong arms around me, your smooth body close to mine — your kisses on my ——"

Sue Shut up, Matthew. God! My face is going red. Why did you keep them?

Henry I've told you.

Matthew That's not the reason. He couldn't let you go, Mum. That's why he kept the picture.

Henry It was in a drawer.

Sue I can't believe I wrote letters like these ...

Henry Can't you? They get funnier.

Sue Funnier?

Henry (*enjoying himself*) Have you got to the one where you say: "Whenever I hear them say your name my heart quickens, and the colour comes to my face at the thought of the secrets we share ... "

Sue Not in front of Matthew.

Henry Why not? He's learning something tonight.

Sue The only thing he's learning is never to put pen to paper. Why didn't you destroy them?

Matthew Like you did, Mum?

Sue What?

Matthew takes some letters from his haversack and hands them to Sue

Henry's laughter dies

Henry What are those?

Matthew Your letters to Mum.

Sue They were in the loft! What are you doing with them?

Matthew I didn't want Terry to find them. You know how jealous he can be.

Henry You kept my letters?

Sue I'd forgotten about them. Not that it mattered. They're not very revealing. Your father was always circumspect. Listen. (*Reading*) "Last night I almost said those three little words. I think you know the words I mean. Only caution prevented me from going further." (*She breaks off*) It's a pity caution didn't prevent you going further in other ways. Ah, here it is. (*Reading*) "We must be careful. I have a friend who may be able to provide me with a certain item; if not, there's mail order, although I am worried about using my home address. Possibly, I may be able to find a little shop somewhere on the other side of town ... Wish me luck. Until tomorrow night. Yours, Burma."

Matthew Burma? Why did you call yourself Burma?

Sue Your father always wrote in code. That was in case my parents found the letters. He didn't want to be implicated in anything. Unfortunately they were the only precautions he did take. The chemists never understood his veiled requests and he usually came away with a bottle of aspirins.

Matthew smiles

Henry Will you stop smirking, Matthew? Go and have another go at the car.

Matthew exits, grinning

Sue (*with a worried frown*) Suppose he can't start it?
Henry You could go to a hotel.
Sue I can't afford a hotel.
Henry (*loftily*) I could stay at a first-class hotel for the rest of my life.
Sue Really?
Henry Well, as long as I died at eighty-seven.
Sue You worked it out? How like you. (*Pause*) I suppose I could go to Maisie Coupland.
Henry You wouldn't get a warm welcome there.
Sue Why not? She's my oldest friend.
Henry She's never forgiven you for the way you treated me.
Sue How do you know?
Henry I meet her in the supermarket. She says she doesn't know how I stuck it for so long.
Sue The hypocrite.
Henry Her sympathies are entirely with me.
Sue They're not. She still writes. She says she often sees you in Tesco's — looking for bargains. She says you're as mean as ever.
Henry The devious bat! I don't know why I'm surprised. All your friends were like that in the wife-swapping circle. Well, if you're so close to Maisie Coupland you'd better go to her.
Sue (*looking at her watch*) I don't think I dare — not at this time of night. (*Pause*) I suppose I could tell Terry I'd stayed at Maisie's ...
Henry And do what?
Sue (*after a hesitation*) Stay here.
Henry Well, well, well.
Sue Don't start that again.
Henry I suppose I could move the apples out of the little room for Matthew. Christine could stay where she is — and you could sleep in my bed.
Sue What?
Henry You've done it before.
Sue (*frowning*) Henry.
Henry Don't worry. I'll sleep here, on the couch, fighting temptation with my nails digging into my palms and thinking desperately of healthy walks and cold showers.

Sue Stop it. (*She studies him*) Do you know something? You've never lost that sneer, have you?

Henry I don't sneer.

Sue You do. You should be careful. It's becoming fixed. I can just hear the undertaker saying: "We got him into the coffin all right but I'm afraid we couldn't remove the sneer."

Henry I'm not sneering. I'm merely amused at the way things have turned out, that's all.

There is the sound again of the car failing to start. Sue and Henry listen. Then there is silence

Sue It won't start.

Henry No.

Sue What do you think the neighbours will say?

Henry About what?

Sue A woman staying the night.

Henry It's happened before.

Sue Has it?

Henry In fact, it's a regular event.

Sue Oh. So they're used to it?

Henry Oh, yes. My neighbours are broad-minded. As long as you don't park on their verge, they don't worry. Perhaps you'd like to use the bathroom first — to save any embarrassment.

Matthew enters

Matthew Can't do anything with it — it's buggered.

Henry Don't use that language here. It may be everyday speech where you come from — even a term of affection — but not here. Now, go to the little bedroom and move the apples into the loft.

Matthew We're staying!

Henry Just for tonight. So don't put any posters up.

Matthew Right! (*He heads for the exit*)

Christine enters wearing her coat over her shoulders

Matthew stops. Christine shivers and whispers in his ear

Matthew Of course. (*To Henry*) Could Christine have a hot water bottle?

Henry (*bleakly*) Kitchen — bottom drawer.

Matthew Thanks.

Matthew and Christine exit

Henry Why does she have to shiver like that?

Sue She's cold.

Henry You don't go into other people's houses and shiver. She's doing it to annoy me. (*Pause*) When you've finished in the bathroom, could you leave my pyjamas in there? You'll find them under the pillow. I'll get some blankets ...

Sue rearranges the cushions on the couch during the following

Sue Are you sure you'll be comfortable?

Henry Perfectly.

Sue (*after a hesitation*) Is there something for me to wear?

Henry Oh, you've taken to wearing something?

Sue Yes.

Henry That's new. (*Smiling*) You didn't used to be so formal. I've just remembered what Burma stood for. It wasn't an alias ...

Sue (*clutching a cushion almost defensively*) Wasn't it?

Henry You know it wasn't. It was short for, "Be undressed and ready, my angel."

Sue throws the cushion at him and exits

(*Plumping the cushion and smiling*) Well, well, well ...

CURTAIN

ACT II
Scene 1

The same. Midnight

When the Curtain *rises the room is lit just by the faint light of the table lamp*

Henry, in his shirt and trousers, is trying to sleep on the makeshift bed on the couch. He moves restlessly and eventually rolls off the couch on to the floor. He stands up and switches on the main light. He takes the loose change from his back pocket and moves to the jar on the bookcase. He is about to drop the money in when he realizes the jar is empty. He frowns, drops the money in the jar, switches off the main light and returns to the couch. He switches off the table light

A Light comes on in the hall

Matthew enters, fully dressed and shivering, from the hall. He moves to the drinks tray

Henry watches Matthew; Matthew becomes aware of Henry. Henry switches on the table lamp

Matthew What are you doing down here?
Henry Trying to sleep.
Matthew I've given up. It's cold in that little bedroom — and damp.
Henry The apples like it. What did you come down for?
Matthew (*after a hesitation*) A smoke.
Henry Not in here.
Matthew I was going into the conservatory.
Henry You're not smoking amongst my tomatoes.
Matthew A little smoke won't hurt.
Henry Tell your lungs that. Forty years ago I worked in an office.
Matthew (*wearily*) I know.
Henry All the smokers are dead.
Matthew (*raising the decanter*) And the drinkers.
Henry Yes. But they lived longer. The reason being that the liver is a sturdier organ than the lungs.
Matthew (*replacing the decanter*) I must say I'm surprised you're down here.

Henry Why?

Matthew Thought you might be up there …

Henry What are you suggesting?

Matthew Nothing …

Henry Oh yes, you are. That lady is another man's wife. Apart from which, I haven't exactly fallen apart in her absence, nor have I pined for her return. I admit it was a shock when she went but I've got over that. My name's Willows. I may bend a little but I don't break.

Matthew I haven't noticed you bending that much. (*Pause*) They wanted me to change my name.

Henry (*unimpressed*) Did they?

Matthew But I wouldn't. I said Willows is my name and always will be. I was born a Willows and I'll die a Willows. I said ——

Henry Matthew, stop creeping. (*Pause*) Do you know why I couldn't sleep? Loose change in my back pocket.

Matthew You shouldn't carry loose change in your pockets — it damages the lining.

Henry It doesn't stay in your pocket long enough to damage the lining. Do you remember what I used to do with it?

Matthew No.

Henry I'd put it in that jar …

Matthew You did that, too, did you?

Henry (*staring*) What?

Matthew That's what I did. I stopped in the end.

Henry Why?

Matthew It kept disappearing.

Henry (*angrily*) It disappeared tonight.

Matthew Never mind. It's only money. Money's never been my god.

Henry It isn't mine! Are you suggesting it's mine?

Matthew No.

Henry Let me tell you something about yourself — just in case you don't know. It's not money you despise — it's working for it. Now get to bed.

Matthew heads for the door, then pauses

Matthew Are you staying down here?

Henry Of course I'm staying down here. Aren't you forgetting something? We're divorced.

Matthew Tell the Pope that.

Henry I'm not a Catholic! Matthew, our relationship is over. You're the one who's related to that woman up there — not me. I have no more in common with her than the woman on the check-out at Tesco's.

Matthew Have you been seeing her?

Henry (*staring*) Who?

Matthew The woman on the check-out?
Henry No! I am making a point. You can marry someone with the best of
intentions — and then, years later, you wake up in bed with a total stranger.

Matthew nods thoughtfully

Matthew Was that the woman from Tesco's?
Henry No!

Matthew makes to leave

Your mother says you've been suspended from college?
Matthew (*stopping*) Yes.
Henry When are you going back?
Matthew I may not go back. I may have to get a job. I need money.
Henry I thought that was a commodity you despised?
Matthew I do. But I have responsibilities now. I have to live by the rules of
society. And they've taken my credit card away.
Henry That must have been a blow.
Matthew It was. I'm lost without our flexible friend.
Henry It's a plastic dream world, Matthew. I never use them.
Matthew I did. All the time. It's so humiliating to be without one. I was at
the Lotus House the other night, with Christine and the rest. She had a
Barclaycard, Gary had American Express, Jenny had Access. And there I
was wondering if I had enough cash left for a banana fritter. I almost had
nervous indigestion.
Henry But don't you see? You couldn't have what you couldn't afford. You
had to cut your cloth according to your means.
Matthew I still had the banana fritter.
Henry Let me tell you a little story. When I was young — younger than
Christine — I saw a suit in Burton's window. I really wanted that suit. But
I couldn't afford it. So I went down to the market and found some wood,
got some wheels off an old pram, and made a little truck. Then I sawed up
some logs and sold firewood from door to door. It took a long time but I
got the money. And when I bought that suit, do you know what I found?
Matthew It was out of fashion.
Henry No. It meant more to me than any suit I've bought since.
Matthew There's not much call for firewood these days. I can't afford to
study. I'll have to get a job. (*Slyly*) Things may have been different if
Grandad Willows had remembered me ...
Henry (*after a pause*) He did remember you.
Matthew What!
Henry Don't get excited. It wasn't a bequest. But he always had a soft spot
for you. And as a personal favour to him he asked me to give you ...

Matthew What?

Henry Ten thousand.

Matthew Ten thousand! Wow!

Henry There were conditions. That you pursued your studies diligently. That you grew up decent and respectable.

Matthew Yes?

Henry Sober and industrious ——

Matthew Yes?

Henry — and responsible ——

Matthew He said all that?

Henry Yes.

Matthew You haven't added anything?

Henry No.

Matthew I'm not going to get it, am I?

Henry I'm still thinking about it. Why were you suspended from college?

Matthew I led a raid on the science lab.

Henry Why?

Matthew To release some mice. They were experimenting on them. We were seen. We all wore Balaclavas but I wore a distinctive T-shirt …

Henry How distinctive?

Matthew Che Guevara.

Henry Matthew, if you're going to get involved in anything so ridiculous couldn't you have worn a plain vest?

Matthew It's not ridiculous. They may be mice, but they're God's creatures.

Henry Read your Bible, Matthew. "Let man have dominion over the fish of the sea and fowl of the air and over the cattle and all the earth and every creeping thing that creepeth on the earth."

Matthew That doesn't mean we have to be cruel to them.

Henry You don't even like animals. You never did. You don't like them licking you.

Matthew Well, no but ——

Henry You wouldn't even walk the dog.

Matthew We haven't got a dog. We've never had a dog.

Henry If we had a dog, you wouldn't walk it.

Matthew Now I'm getting the blame for not walking a dog we haven't got! All right I don't like them licking me. I still wouldn't eat them. That's why I'm a vegetarian.

Henry Vegetarian! You don't eat vegetables. You'd faint at the sight of a Brussel. How can you be a vegetarian if you don't eat greens?

Matthew Well, I don't eat meat either.

Henry You would if you were hungry enough. If you were adrift in an open boat you'd eat meat. You'd eat the soles off your shoes and probably the cabin boy — anything to stay alive.

Matthew I wouldn't eat a cabin boy.

Henry And you smoke.

Matthew What's that got to do with it?

Henry Don't tobacco companies experiment on dogs?

Matthew Yes.

Henry If you smokers gave up in protest — they'd stop.

Matthew That's different.

Henry No — you'd sooner wear a Balaclava helmet and frighten people. But when you've got them frightened you have to keep them frightened. Once you've put on that Balaclava you'll never be able to take it off.

Matthew All right. I'll stop smoking on one condition.

Henry What's that?

Matthew That you lose weight.

Henry I don't need to lose weight.

Matthew No woman's going to look at a man who's two stone overweight.

Henry Two stone!

Matthew That's like carrying a bag of potatoes around with you. When you go upstairs you're carrying a bag of potatoes. Every time you go to bed — so does your bag of potatoes. That's what everyone's thinking — there goes Henry Willows and his bag of potatoes. And one day, if you're not careful, you'll look like a bag of potatoes.

Henry I won't.

Matthew It's so ageing, Mr Willows. Terry hasn't put on a pound.

Henry I'm not interested in Terry.

Matthew You should go on a diet.

Henry (*after a hesitation*) I don't know. I should need to see a doctor first.

Matthew Why?

Henry You're supposed to seek medical advice before you take weight off.

Matthew Why? You didn't seek medical advice before you put it on. You'd look so much better, Mr Willows.

Henry Stop calling me that.

Matthew You mean I should call you Dad? You don't mind people knowing?

Henry No. After all, you can't choose your relatives. (*Pause*) Why do you want me to look better?

Matthew No reason. I just want a good-looking dad ... (*He moves to the hall door*) Well, good-night, Dad. (*Pause*) Oh, about the ten thousand ...

Henry Yes?

Matthew What about the interest?

Henry Get to bed!

Matthew exits

Henry pulls in his stomach thoughtfully then returns to the couch and settles down. He switches off the lamp. There is a moment's pause

Sue enters wearing Henry's winceyette pyjamas and a topcoat. She moves to the drinks tray

Henry switches on the lamp

Sue (*turning*) Before you say, "Well, well, well": I'm frozen. I need something to warm me.
Henry (*grinning*) Really?
Sue Stop grinning. I'd forgotten how cold that bedroom could be.
Henry It's healthy.
Sue It's cheap. I was shivering. I always did. And you always had the windows open. One winter I woke up covered in snow.
Henry I kept you warm, didn't I?
Sue That's more than the central heating did. Our fuel bills were the lowest on the road.
Henry We had to be careful in those days.
Sue There's a difference between being careful and being mean.
Henry I was not mean! I was careful. I spent less on myself than anyone.
Sue I didn't say you were greedy — I said you were mean. There's a difference. Terry's greedy but he's not mean.
Henry He's certainly one of life's takers. He took everything I had. And he's been married three times.
Sue Twice. You always got that wrong. (*She lifts the decanter*)
Henry I wouldn't drink that.
Sue Is it rationed?
Henry No — it's vinegar.
Sue (*staring*) You're drinking vinegar?
Henry It's for Matthew. He's been helping himself.
Sue You don't change, Henry.
Henry Neither does Matthew. Try the brandy.

Sue pours herself a brandy

He says Frank's been wetting the bed ...

Sue sips her drink

Sue Sometimes.
Henry What do you mean — sometimes?
Sue Often. I have to lift him, or Matthew does. They share.
Henry Why do you think he does that?
Sue I don't know. Matthew will tell him these bedtime stories. "The Night of the Werewolves", or "The Revenge of the Flesh-Eating Zombies". Anything with mutations in it. Now Frank's always waiting for people to mutate — even me.

Henry I thought you already had.

Sue (*ignoring this*) It makes for disturbed nights.

Henry What about tonight?

Sue I don't know. I should be there. Terry does his best but Frank's not his son.

Henry Does he hit him?

Sue Frank can be very rude.

Henry And you wonder why he wets the bed — why he's rude! (*Pause*) I want you to do something for me. I want you to tell Terry, in a quiet and reasonable voice, so he knows you're serious, that if he lays a hand on Frank again, I'll come up there and tear his frigging head off.

Sue (*staring at him*) I don't think you can say that in a quiet and reasonable voice, Henry. (*She shivers*)

Henry Will you stop shivering! I don't like the way people come to my house and shiver!

Sue Then turn up the heat.

Henry Have some more brandy. (*He moves to her*)

Sue No — it'll make my heart race.

Henry (*archly*) You mean, it's not racing already? (*He opens her coat slightly*) With just the thickness of winceyette between us?

Sue Don't be flirtatious, Henry. It doesn't suit you. It's like watching an elephant dance.

Henry (*frowning*) An elephant. Do you think I've put on weight?

Sue I hadn't noticed. I certainly have.

Henry It's not keeping you warm.

Sue No.

Henry Share these blankets — until you're warm enough …

Sue hesitates and then sits on the couch. Henry sits and puts the blankets around her

Sue It's not very comfortable. I suppose you miss your bed.

Henry Yes. I've discovered that the one joy of being single is that you can sleep diagonally.

Sue I didn't know that.

Henry But then you always liked to snuggle up.

Sue I was afraid of the dark.

Henry I like the dark.

Sue So did Dracula.

Henry Winter evenings — glass of Scotch — a roaring fire …

Sue Your fire never roared.

Henry Funny. I like the night — you like the day. I like winter — you like summer. Surprised we ever got together.

Sue (*shrugging*) Even hedgehogs mate.

Henry Now I'm a hedgehog. Is that how you see me?

Sue No. Why are you suddenly worried about your looks? You never used to be.

Henry That's when I had them. And what about you? You used to take your make-up off at night.

Sue I still do.

Henry Not tonight.

Sue I thought it might keep me warm.

Henry I'll keep you warm.

Sue Henry, don't. Things are different now.

Henry In what way?

Sue I'm married.

Henry You were married before — it never stopped you.

Sue It's stopping me now.

Henry Matthew says we're still married in the eyes of God.

Sue But not in the eye of Leeds registry office.

Henry He has precedence.

Sue Not in Leeds. Henry, I don't feel married to you.

Henry I know — exciting, isn't it? (*He kisses her and then studies her for a moment*) Your lips are warmer than I remember. Trouble is, memory's turned you into a statue.

Sue You mean unfeeling?

Henry You were never that. (*He kisses her again*)

Sue Stop it, Hen.

Henry (*smiling*) Hen. No-one's called me that in a long time.

Sue Not any of those women who've been wearing a groove in your bedroom carpet?

Henry No. Hen was special ...

Sue (*breaking away*) Why couldn't you have been more practical?

Henry Why?

Sue You could have fixed the car.

Henry He should have bought you a decent car.

Sue It's not been easy raising three children. And your contribution hasn't been exactly lavish. And now Julie's into clothes.

Henry Is she attractive?

Sue Very.

Henry I thought she would be.

Sue I don't want her to grow up too fast.

Henry Of course you don't — not if you're still trying to pass for thirty-five.

Sue She wants to go on the pill.

Henry What! (*He leaps to his feet*) The pill! At her age?

Sue Don't shout. She says it's her body.

Henry Her body? She's only just got it!

Sue Apparently all her friends are on it.

Henry (*drily*) All of them? Surely one or two are still holding out.

Sue Not according to Julie. And you know how stubborn she can be.

Henry Is she in a relationship?

Sue Well, she has a special boyfriend. Paul. He's a very nice boy. I don't think it's a relationship.

Henry Then why does she want to go on the pill?

Sue Julie says you wear a seat belt but that doesn't mean you expect an accident.

Henry It means you drive faster. She's only got one body — it's important to her. One day it's going to be important to somebody else, and she'll be a physical wreck. Tell her I forbid it.

Sue I don't think you can. Besides, they want to go on a camping holiday.

Henry What!

The phone rings, off

Sue The phone's ringing.

Henry Let it ring. Where are they going?

Sue France.

Henry France! In a tent?

Sue That's what it usually means.

Henry A strip of canvas between her and the Gallic hordes?

Sue Paul will be with her.

Henry In a tent?

Sue In sleeping bags.

Henry I forbid it. (*He moves to the door*)

The phone stops ringing

Sue You can't.

Henry I can. I'm her father.

Sue Isn't it a little late? You've never shown any interest before. Now she's becoming a young lady, it's different.

Henry And attractive … ?

Sue Yes.

Henry And she's alone with Terry — the three-time loser.

Sue Two times. And what are you getting at?

Henry Get your clothes on. I'm driving you back.

Sue What?

There are sounds, off, of someone approaching

Henry Someone's coming.

Henry pushes Sue back under the blankets

Matthew enters

Matthew That was Terry.
Henry What did he want?
Matthew He wanted to know where Mum was.
Henry What did you say?
Matthew I put his mind at rest. I told him she was safe with us.

Sue groans faintly

Henry (*quickly*) What did he say?
Matthew He made a sort of choking sound.
Henry Wake Christine and tell her to get dressed. I'm driving you back.
Matthew Why?
Henry (*lowering his voice*) Because Frank and Julie are alone with him.
Matthew They're not.
Henry (*staring*) What?
Matthew They're sleeping over at Paul's. I arranged it with Paul's Mum. I
    thought if we were going to be here …
Henry You arranged it?
Matthew Yes.
Henry (*suspiciously*) That was very far-sighted of you.
Matthew I like to anticipate events.
Henry I can see that. (*Pause*) Did Terry say anything else?
Matthew Yes. He said if Mum stays here tonight — she needn't bother to
    come back.
Henry Oh. (*Pause*) Well, there's no point in dashing back now. I'll get the
    car fixed tomorrow.
Matthew Right, night, Dad.
Henry Good-night.

Matthew exits

Sue rises from beneath the blankets

Sue Oh, my God! Why did he have to tell him?
Henry Did you expect anything less? Remember the roll-neck sweater
    incident?

Sue You'd better take me back.

Henry At this time of night?

Sue You were going to.

Henry That was when I thought my children were alone with a monster.

Sue He's not a monster.

Henry Then you've got nothing to worry about. He'll forgive you. After all, we're doing nothing wrong.

Sue Aren't we?

Henry No.

Sue We're sharing a couch.

Henry So what? It's perfectly respectable. I've shared this couch with the vicar before now.

Sue Not in pyjamas.

Henry You don't have to tell him that. Just deny everything — like you did with me. I believed you.

Sue There's nothing to deny! (*Pause*) I just wonder …

Henry What?

Sue If you're not trying to get your own back.

Henry If you mean revenge — no. If you mean getting back what I once had — yes. You'll notice I didn't say "what was once mine". You were never mine, were you?

Sue Henry ——

Henry Shush!

The door opens. Henry pushes Sue out of sight

Matthew half-leads Christine into the room

Matthew Could Christine have some tonic water? Her stomach's upset.

Henry (*briefly*) On the tray.

Matthew (*moving to the tray and pouring a glass of tonic*) She's living on tonic water these days …

Henry Is she?

Matthew returns to Christine. He gives her the tonic and she whispers in his ear

Matthew Oh, and could she have some biscuits? They usually help.

Henry In the kitchen.

Matthew and Christine head for the exit

Matthew Right. Night, Dad. (*He turns at the door*) Night, Mum.

They exit

Sue (*sitting up*) That's torn it. Do you think he'll tell Terry?

Henry He's your son. What do you think?

Sue He's your son too.

Henry I sometimes wonder. You don't think there was some dreadful mix-up at the maternity hospital, do you?

Sue He wouldn't tell Terry, would he?

Henry Anyone who can kick a man's hubcaps in is capable of almost anything.

Sue That was his cousin Nigel.

Henry But who persuaded his cousin Nigel it was a good idea? Tell me that. Didn't he persuade his cousin Nigel he could fly — and didn't Nigel fly straight out of the bedroom window?

Sue He was only a boy.

Henry Only a boy! That was always your excuse. He's never been only a boy. I knew there was something wrong at the christening. The church was bathed in sunshine and full of flowers. It was a haven of peace until the vicar picked him up and he started screaming. Then the sun, that was streaming through the window a moment before, disappeared behind a cloud and the church became cold and dark. I always thought that was an omen.

Sue I'll have to go.

Henry You can't. It's too late. (*He holds her close — more closely than before*)

Sue What are you doing?

Henry Keeping you warm.

Sue Well, don't.

Henry (*after a pause*) When you said Terry was greedy, that was the first time I'd heard you criticize him. (*Pause*) You're not happy, are you?

Sue (*after a hesitation*) No. But I wasn't happy here. (*Pause*) What about you?

Henry I've been miserable.

Sue You always were.

Henry Not as miserable. (*Shrugging*) Perhaps no-one's happy — just less miserable. (*Pause*) What did you mean by greedy?

Sue Nothing.

Henry There have been others — haven't there?

Silence

I thought so.

Sue As you say, I made my choice.

Henry Then he's no right to be jealous.

Sue It doesn't work like that.

Henry No. So whatever we do, he'll think I'm holding and kissing you right
now … (*He nuzzles her*)

Sue What are you doing?

Henry Surely your memory's not that bad.

Sue Don't.

Henry There's a very old and very wise saying. One may as well be hanged
for a sheep as a lamb …

Sue (*standing*) I think the lamb is more than enough for one evening. I'm
going to bed.

Henry Take my blankets — they'll keep you warm.

Sue What about you?

Henry I'll manage …

Sue moves to the door. She looks back nervously

Henry gives a sudden, loud bleat

Sue quickens her step and exits

Henry smiles and follows her off

CURTAIN

SCENE 2

The same. Late morning, the following day

*The barometer is missing from the wall and Sue's bag and Matthew's
haversack have been set*

*Henry enters in shirtsleeves. He looks ruffled and tired but his mood is sunny.
He feeds the fish*

Henry Sorry breakfast is a little late …

Matthew enters. His shirt is open and he's mopping his brow

Matthew Have you done something to the heating? I'm sweating my balls
off.

Henry Matthew!

Matthew Sorry. But it's sweltering.

Henry I know. Don't ever shiver in my house again.

Matthew regards him curiously

Matthew You're late. It's almost lunchtime.

Henry (*after a hesitation*) I overslept …

Matthew You must have done.

Henry I couldn't sleep on the couch.

Matthew No.

Henry So when your mother got out — I went back to bed …

Matthew Ah.

Henry Where is your mother?

Matthew At the car.

Henry And dear Christine?

Matthew In the kitchen. Trying to eat something.

Henry Of course. She must keep her strength up.

Matthew Yes. (*He takes a tie out of his haversack*) Well, wish me luck.

Henry Why?

Matthew I'm going for an interview.

Henry What?

Matthew Life's moved on since you went to bed, Dad. The world doesn't owe me a living. If I'm staying here, I need to pay my way.

Henry Who says you're staying here?

Matthew Well, I am, aren't I?

Henry (*slowly*) You could be …

Matthew Well, I need to earn some money — that means a job.

Henry What sort of job?

Matthew Wine bar. It was in the local paper. I rang up. It's waiting on, clearing away — that sort of thing. He says if I'm satisfactory he'll set me on straight away.

Henry I see. What are you going to say to him?

Matthew That depends on what he asks me.

Henry He'll ask you why you want the job.

Matthew For the money.

Henry That's your first mistake. Don't mention money — it's a delicate subject.

Matthew It's the truth.

Henry The dole queues are full of people who told the truth.

Matthew What should I say?

Henry Say you've always wanted to work in catering — and you've liked the look of this particular establishment — and you know you'd be happy here.

Matthew I don't even know where it is.

Henry That doesn't matter. (*Pause*) Do you have any special skills? He may ask you that.

Silence

Well, say something.

Matthew I don't think you need any special skills — working in a wine bar.

Henry That's great! You've just told someone who's probably worked in the trade all his life that he has no special skills — that anyone could do his job. You've just made a mockery of his whole existence.

Matthew I never thought of it like that.

Henry Just remember — no matter how menial the job it can always be done quicker and better. He may offer you a cigarette.

Matthew Thanks.

Henry Don't take it.

Matthew Why not?

Henry It could be a ploy. Say you do smoke, but only in moderation and never near food. (*Pause*) Drink?

Matthew No, thanks.

Henry Come on! The man's just offered you a drink. Be sociable.

Matthew It could be a ploy.

Henry So?

Matthew Thanks. I like a drink but only in moderation and never near food.

Henry What?

Matthew I mean, never when I'm working.

Henry That's better. You're learning.

Matthew I've got a good teacher. That's what I've missed, Dad. Being able to talk to someone, someone who knows — who's been around the block a few times. I've missed that. It wasn't the same back there …

Matthew exits into the hall

Flattered, Henry smiles, and then his features lapse into a suspicious frown. He moves to the clock, sets the hands and listens to the tick

Sue enters from the hall wearing a coat which she immediately throws off

Henry (*smiling*) Warm enough for you?

Sue Yes. I'm baking.

Henry Where have you been? I woke and you were gone — and there wasn't even a rose on the pillow.

Sue I've been trying to start the car.

Henry (*staring*) You're going back?

Sue Of course I'm going back.

Henry After last night?

Sue That was last night. I see you've put the clock back.

Henry (*archly*) I thought we did that last night …

Sue Don't sweet talk me, Henry. It won't last, and you know it. When I woke up this morning I felt ashamed.

Henry (*grinning*) Don't you mean sheepish … ?

Sue No. Ashamed.

Henry You weren't ashamed the last time.

Sue Yes. I was.

Henry I put the clock back because I thought you were staying. (*He picks up Sue's bag*) Look, they're yours — I don't want them. (*As he mentions them, he stuffs items into Sue's bag*) Here's the clock, the Dresden shepherdess, the "Sheep Dip" — and *Oliver Twist*. You can have them. If it didn't mean anything. If it's come down to things …

Sue Henry, it did mean something but ——

Henry But you're walking out. So what's new? You walked out before.

Sue Do you know why I walked out before? I wasn't going to. Do you remember the last thing you said to me, before I went?

Henry No.

Sue I was going to give us one last chance. You were being nice to me that night. I said I was going to have a shower. You know what that meant.

Henry Yes. You always had a shower before …

Sue Yes. Do you remember what you said when I said I was going to take a shower?

Henry No.

Sue You said, "Go easy on the hot water." At that moment a little iron entered my soul, Henry.

Henry That's all changed. Go to the meter cupboard — the dials are whizzing round.

Sue How do you know? Have you sat there watching them? You can't change things just by turning up the heat.

Henry But you can't go. The car won't start.

Sue I've asked one of your neighbours to look at it. He said he knew something about cars …

Henry Sue, he doesn't want you back. You heard what Matthew said.

Sue I can't stay here. There's Julie and Frank …

Henry I've been thinking about that. I could move the apples into the loft. If Matthew and Christine got married they could have the middle room …

Sue And Julie?

Henry She could share with you. Frank could have the little room.

Sue And what about you? On the couch? It didn't work too well the last time.

Henry We could build an extension. I've got plans drawn up.

Sue You had plans drawn up twenty years ago, Henry.

Henry Matthew's getting a job — at a wine bar. He can't leave now.

Sue He's not working in a wine bar. He's going back to college. I want him to get his degree.

Henry All right. They can go into student accommodation. I'll pay.

Sue It's too late, Henry.

Henry It's never too late. The sun's shining — see, the outlook's fair ... (*He goes to tap at the barometer and then realizes it's missing from the wall. His expression changes*) All right. Where is it?

Sue What?

Henry The barometer. And don't say it's yours because it isn't. Where is it — in the car? Is that why you got up early — for a quick get-away? This isn't a visit — it's a raid. I'm surprised you've left the towels. It's come down to things with you, hasn't it?

Sue No.

Henry Well, that barometer belonged to my father. A similar one was highly valued on *Antiques Roadshow*. And you're not getting away with that.

Sue I'm not trying to.

Henry What?

Sue I didn't take it. Henry. I don't need a barometer to tell me the outlook around here — it's invariably stormy and usually overcast. I'll see if he's fixed the car.

Sue exits

Henry stares after her blankly for a moment and then the realization dawns

Henry Matthew!

Matthew enters wearing a coat

Matthew Yes, Dad.

Henry Don't call me that.

Matthew What?

Henry What have you done with my barometer?

Matthew Don't you mean my barometer?

Henry Your barometer? That barometer belonged to my father.

Matthew I know. He said he wanted me to have it.

Henry When did he say that?

Matthew Towards the end. Whenever I was passing by his place, I visited.

Henry I didn't know that.

Matthew We were very close. He was my grandfather.

Henry Yes, but that barometer's valuable.

Matthew I always tapped it before I left — and I'd say, "Outlook sunny, Gramps."

Henry Gramps?

Matthew That's what I called him. He liked that. The last time I saw him — I think he knew it was near the end — he put his hand on mine and said: "Matthew, you're the first born of my first born and I want you to have that barometer."

Henry He never talked like that.

Matthew He did towards the end. He said "When I'm gone you'll be able to tap that barometer and think of me" — because we always looked at that barometer together.

Henry (*moved*) He really said that?

Matthew Yes. (*Sighing*) Grandad Willows.

Henry (*reflectively*) Yes.

Matthew Nice old man.

Henry Salt of the earth.

Matthew They don't make them like him any more.

Henry No. (*Pause*) What are you going to do with it?

Matthew Sell it.

Henry What! I thought it had sentimental value?

Matthew I can't afford to be sentimental. I have responsibilities now.

Henry (*sighing*) All right. You win. You can put that barometer back. (*He moves to the sideboard and takes a cheque book and pen from the drawer*)

Matthew What are you going to do?

Henry (*writing a cheque*) I'm making out a cheque — for half Grandad's money. There are conditions. One, that you return to college as soon as possible.

Matthew Why?

Henry Because it's your mother's wish. The other condition is that you spend the money only on essentials.

Matthew Don't worry — this is going straight into the bank. (*He takes the cheque and brandishes it*) This should raise a few eyebrows down there.

Henry (*drily*) Oh. I don't know — I suppose they've come across a few in their time.

Matthew I think I'll get that credit card with the four million outlets world-wide. I'll have a cheque book in a leather wallet. Oh, and a direct debit card as well …

Henry Matthew, don't get carried away. I want to see how you handle this.

Matthew Don't worry. I'm going to be level-headed, Dad. I've seen too much poverty in my life. Either you work for money or money works for you — and I know what I prefer.

Henry I can imagine.

Matthew I want to be like you, Dad. You can earn your money whilst you're asleep.

Henry What?

Matthew That's what I want to do. Oh, and talking of essentials, you don't mind if we buy a pram?

Henry A pram?

Matthew It could stand in the hall.

Henry (*weakly*) A pram in the hall?

Matthew There's room for it.

Henry Matthew, you're not staying.

Matthew What?

Henry Your mother's leaving.

Matthew You're letting her go again?

Henry I didn't let her go the first time. She went.

Matthew And what's she going back to? Have you thought of that? Reproaches and accusations — possibly violence.

Henry She seems to prefer that to here.

Matthew And what about Julie and Frank? Have you thought about them? Julie growing up far too fast and slapping make-up on an inch thick — and Frank's mattress becoming more and more like Hackney Marshes. They need you — we all do.

Henry studies Matthew for a moment

Henry It won't work, Matthew. You can't wind me up any more — it's too late. Your mother's leaving.

Matthew She's not leaving. The car won't start. There's still time to talk to her. Come on, Dad. A few words won't hurt …

Matthew almost propels Henry into the hall

Christine enters

Not now, Christine. Family business …

Matthew and Henry exit leaving Christine alone

Christine picks up her haversack and makes for the conservatory. Her mobile phone rings. She answers it. Her voice is surprisingly middle-class

During the following, Henry and Sue appear at the door and stare incredulously at Christine

Christine Daddy? … Oh, thank God. I want to come home. It's awful here. They're such terrible people. They shout and quarrel. And he's a monster. And there's a likeness. I couldn't marry Matthew. The thought of him becoming more like his father every day — it's too awful. (*Pause*) Daddy, did Mummy tell you why I had to go away? … She did? … Are you sure it doesn't matter? … What about Simon? Has he asked after me? Does he know? … He doesn't care? But I've treated him so badly … Oh, I can't wait to see you all. I've rung the station. There's a train at four. I'll be home at six. I can't stand this place a moment later, they're such … (*Her voice dies away as she catches sight of Sue and Henry*)

Christine snatches up her haversack and dashes out through the conservatory

Silence

Sue Well, she appears to have recovered her voice.
Henry I think I prefer the silence.
Sue She speaks quite nicely, doesn't she?
Henry Speaks quite nicely! Did you hear what she said? What have we done?
Sue What do you mean? What have we done? You're the monster.
Henry What?
Sue But don't blame yourself too much. She was totally wrong for him.
Henry But what are we going to tell him? He was going to buy a pram.
Sue You'll think of something.
Henry What!
Sue After all, you are his father. That's what fathers are for. (*She kisses him lightly on the cheek*) Try and break it gently.
Henry Gently!
Sue I'll send him through.

Sue exits

Henry takes up the fish food and sprinkles some in the tank. He sighs

Henry I wish I had your simple life. Suddenly, just lying there under a stone seems tremendously attractive. What's the matter? Lost your appetite? You wouldn't eat a damned thing if you had my life.

Matthew enters. He looks around

Matthew Where's Christine?
Henry She's not here.
Matthew I can see that. Where is she?
Henry I've got something to tell you.
Matthew What?
Henry You know I'm always saying life's full of disappointments ...?
Matthew Yes?
Henry That youth's a mistake — manhood a struggle — old age a regret?
Matthew Yes?
Henry Well, you've got to regret earlier than most ...
Matthew What do you mean?
Henry It's all part of growing up.
Matthew What is?
Henry Do you remember something else I'm always saying?

Matthew You mean, don't expect too much of people because they'll always let you down?

Henry That's the one.

Matthew What's happened?

Henry Christine's gone. She doesn't love you any more. She doesn't want to see you again.

Matthew Oh.

Henry If it means anything, I'm sorry. (*He pours a glass of Scotch*) Well, I'm not sorry, but I'm sorry. If you know what I mean.

Matthew (*sadly*) I know what you mean.

Henry offers Matthew the Scotch. Matthew shakes his head

Henry I know how you feel about the baby and everything. And we'll face that when the time comes. We'll make arrangements. There'll be visiting — Sundays — trips to the zoo … Things won't be so bad.

Matthew No. If she doesn't want to see me, then that's it.

Henry (*staring*) But the baby …

Matthew I know — but it's not as if it's mine.

Henry (*gaping*) What did you say?

Matthew I said, it's not as if it's mine. I'm not the father, am I?

Henry You're not?

Matthew No. Didn't I make that clear?

Henry Not in as many words. If it's not yours — whose is it?

Matthew Simon's. Happened in the back of his Mondeo — otherwise known as the virgins' hearse.

Henry You mean you were prepared to marry someone who was having another man's child?

Matthew I thought I loved her.

Henry Wait a minute. You thought you loved her?

Matthew Well, I've been rejected, haven't I? I've had my feelings trampled on. I know when I'm not wanted. I'm like you, Dad. I'm a Willows. I may bend but I don't break. If that's the way it is. *Que sera, sera.*

Henry (*weakly*) *Que sera, sera?*

Matthew Whatever will be, will be. And there was another drawback. She didn't like you, Dad. And with me the family always comes first.

Henry It does?

Matthew And there's another good thing to come out of this. There'll be more room for Frank and Julie.

Henry You haven't been listening, Matthew. Your mother won't stay. They're not coming.

Matthew They are. They're on the two o'clock train.

Henry What! (*He takes a deep draught of his drink. He chokes on the vinegar and is unable to speak*)

Matthew I've been on the phone to them. They're not happy, Dad. I said, if they're not happy, they may as well come here and be miserable with you — at least you're their father. I've been thinking — we could take the apples out the loft and put them in the garden shed, then we could put down some boards, put in a window and a staircase — we'd have plenty of room. If you can see any snags, say so.

Henry opens and closes his mouth

You can't, can you? And you know you'll be lonely without us. Especially now the fish is dead.
Henry (*finally recovers his voice*) What did you say?
Matthew It's lying dead under that stone.
Henry Let me see.

They study the fish tank. Henry disturbs the water

You're right.
Matthew I'll get rid of it. It'll only upset you …
Henry (*looking at Matthew suspiciously*) Wait a minute. Let me see that. (*He examines the fish*) This isn't a fish. This is a piece of carrot cut in the shape of a fish. What have you been up to?
Matthew It'll be happier where it is.
Henry Where is it?
Matthew Botanical gardens.
Henry What!
Matthew In the ornamental pond.
Henry That was my fish! He was a pet.
Matthew He'll be happier with all the other fish.
Henry He knew me.
Matthew He didn't know you.
Henry He came to the edge of the tank and looked at me.
Matthew He was looking at his reflection, Dad. And do you know why? Because he was lonely, like you. He wanted to be amongst his own kind.
Henry He came when I called him.
Matthew Well, you can go down to the pond and try it — but I don't think he'll come. Well, I can't stand here all day — I've got to meet the train and bank that cheque. Busy, busy, busy. (*He heads for the hall but pauses*) You don't need that fish any more, Dad — not now you've got us … *Ciao*.

Matthew exits

Henry is about to take another drink, realizes in time that it's vinegar and puts the glass down

Sue enters

Sue Well?

Henry He's liberated my goldfish! I've been feeding a piece of carrot all morning.

Sue He's always been soft-hearted.

Henry You don't know how soft.

Sue How did he take it?

Henry Quite well. But then the child isn't his!

Sue What!

Henry Apparently, it's Simon's — the boy next door. Drives a Mondeo — which is affectionately known as the virgins' hearse.

Sue And Matthew was prepared to stand by her?

Henry He thought he loved her.

Sue Do you know, Henry, we have a very special son.

Henry You can say that again. He's sent for Frank and Julie.

Sue What?

Henry It's open house here. Now he's got rid of the goldfish he says there's room for everyone. I told him you weren't staying but he won't listen. (*Pause*) You are going back?

Sue looks at Henry for a moment

Sue I can't.

Henry What?

Sue I can't go back. The car won't start. Your neighbour looked at it. He said it was impossible. In fact, he didn't know how I got here in the first place.

Henry As bad as that?

Sue Apparently someone removed the leads and you can't start a car without them. I think we know who that someone was ...

Henry We've been Matthewed.

Sue Well, I suppose I'll have to make the best of things.

Henry You're staying?

Sue (*shrugging*) I don't think I'll be very welcome back there. Besides (*smiling*) all my family are here.

Henry You won't regret it. I'll take you out tonight. We'll celebrate. We'll go to the Grange.

Sue The Grange? I've nothing to wear.

Henry Then we'll buy something this afternoon.

Sue It'll have to be good — the Grange is terribly expensive.

Henry (*worriedly*) Is it? Well, we don't have to go *à la carte* ...

Sue What?

Henry (*quickly*) Of course we'll go *à la carte*. We're celebrating.

Sue Can the others come?
Henry What — all of them?
Sue Why not? I'm sure it'll be all right.
Henry Yes. They may do children's portions. (*Quickly*) Not that it matters.
Sue (*smiling*) Are you sure you can keep this up, Henry?
Henry What do you mean?
Sue In the last year we were together we only went out once in the evening
— and that was to vote. Are you sure about this?
Henry Yes.

They kiss. She looks up at him

Sue I think I'll take a shower ...
Henry There's plenty of hot water ...

Sue exits. Henry follows

CURTAIN

FURNITURE AND PROPERTY LIST

ACT I
SCENE 1

On stage: Barometer
Electric fire in fireplace
Radiogram
Sideboard. *On it*: carriage clock; drinks tray with decanter of Scotch, bottle of brandy, tonic water, jug of water, glasses etc.; various photographs including one of a bowls team; fruit bowl containing four bananas; Dresden figurine of a shepherdess; Victorian miniature of a sheep dip. *In bottom drawer*: framed photograph of Sue. *In another drawer*: bundle of letters written in green ink, cheque book, pen
Bookcase. *On it*: books, jar of loose change
Small table. *On it*: fishtank containing single fish, container of fish food
Three piece suite
Coffee table
Newspaper and glass of Scotch for **Henry**

Off stage: Large haversack. In it: tie (**Matthew**)
Large haversack (**Christine**)
Large shoulder bag. *In it*: predictor from pregnancy detector kit (**Sue**)

SCENE 2

Re-set: Carriage clock on coffee table
Dresden figurine and Victorian miniature on sideboard

ACT II
SCENE 1

Set: Blankets on couch

Personal: **Henry**: loose change

SCENE 2

Strike: Blankets
Barometer

Personal: **Christine**: mobile phone

LIGHTING PLOT

Practical fitting required: table lamp
One interior with exterior window backing, hall and conservatory backing. The same throughout

ACT I, Scene 1

To open: General interior lighting including table lamp with covering spot. Evening effect on exterior backing. Hall light on

Cue 1	**Henry** exits into the hall	(Page 2)
	Bring up light in conservatory	

ACT I, Scene 2

To open: General interior lighting including table lamp with covering spot. Evening effect on exterior backing. Hall light on

No cues

ACT II, Scene 1

To open: Faint light of practical table lamp with covering spot

Cue 2	**Henry** switches on the main light	(Page 30)
	Snap on general interior lighting	
Cue 3	**Henry** switches off the main light	(Page 30)
	Snap off general interior lighting	
Cue 4	**Henry** switches off the table lamp	(Page 30)
	Snap off table lamp and covering spot	
Cue 5	Short pause	(Page 30)
	Bring up light in hall	
Cue 6	**Henry** switches on the table lamp	(Page 30)
	Snap on table lamp and covering spot	
Cue 7	**Henry** switches off the table lamp	(Page 34)
	Snap off table lamp and covering spot	

Cue 8   **Henry** switches on the table lamp   (Page 35)
                Snap on table lamp and covering spot

ACT II, SCENE 2

To open: General interior lighting. Late morning effect on exterior backing

No cues

EFFECTS PLOT

ACT I

Cue 1   As Curtain rises   (Page 1)
Classical music from radiogram

Cue 2   When ready   (Page 1)
Doorbell

Cue 3   **Henry** frowns; pause   (Page 1)
Doorbell

Cue 4   **Henry** turns off the music   (Page 1)
Cut music

Cue 5   **Henry** sprinkles fish food in the tank   (Page 1)
Doorbell

Cue 6   **Henry**: "It's down to freezing."   (Page 1)
Doorbell

Cue 7   **Matthew** fills the decanter from the jug   (Page 14)
Sound of car arriving outside

Cue 8   **Sue** moves towards the hall   (Page 17)
*Sound of clock chiming from **Sue**'s bag*

Cue 9   As Scene 2 begins   (Page 18)
Sound of car failing to start

Cue 10   **Henry**: "You must be slipping."   (Page 20)
Phone rings in hall

Cue 11   **Henry**: " ... things have turned out, that's all."   (Page 28)
Sound of car failing to start

ACT II

Cue 12   **Henry**: "What!"   (Page 38)
Phone rings in hall

Cue 13   **Henry** moves to the door   (Page 38)
Cut phone sound

Cue 14   **Christine** makes for the conservatory   (Page 48)
Mobile phone rings

CPSIA information can be obtained
at www.ICGtesting.com
Printed in the USA
BVHW041149110821
614198BV00013B/209